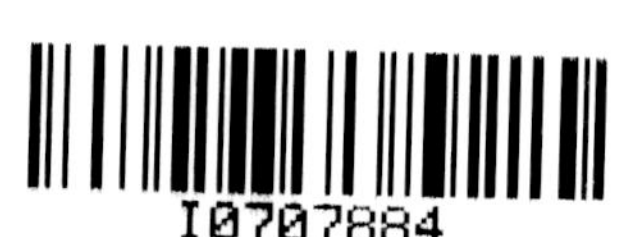

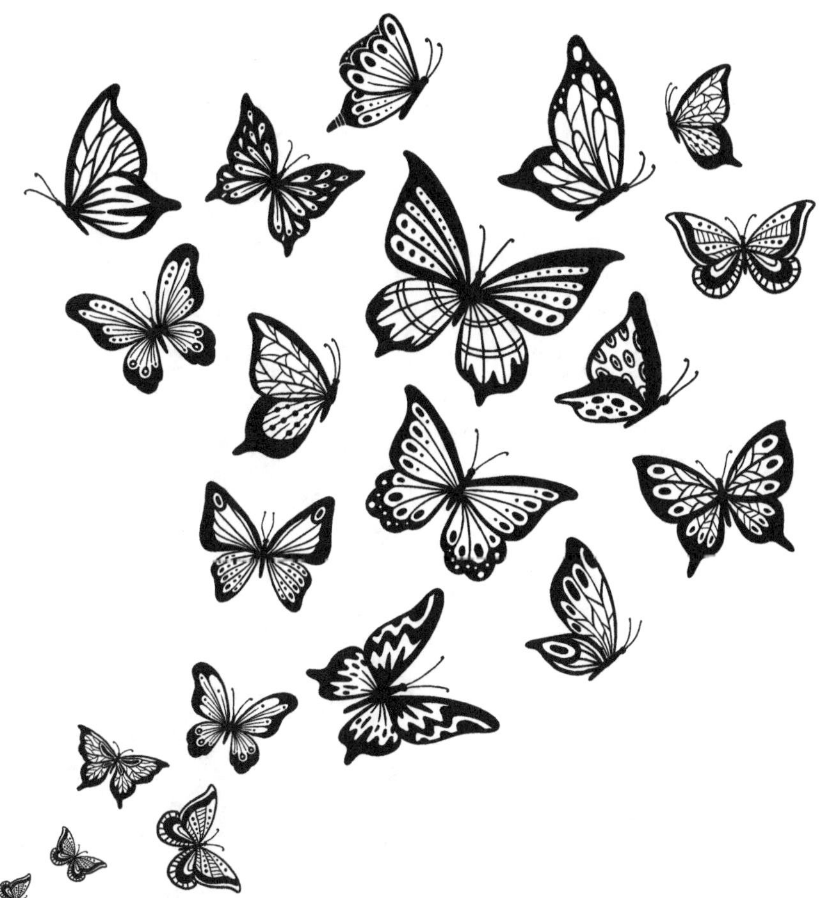

BUTTERFLY

COLORING BOOK

FOR ADULTS

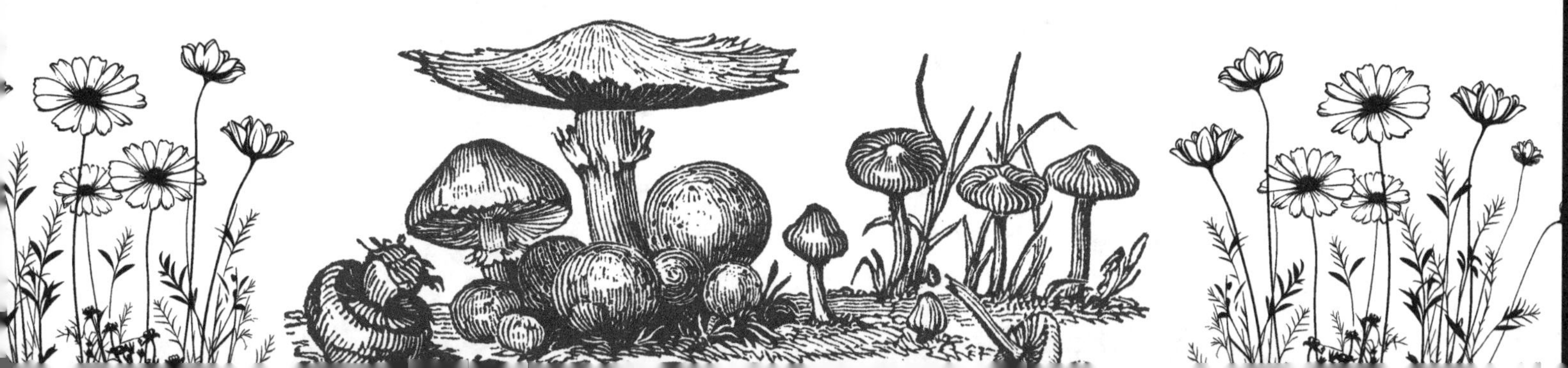

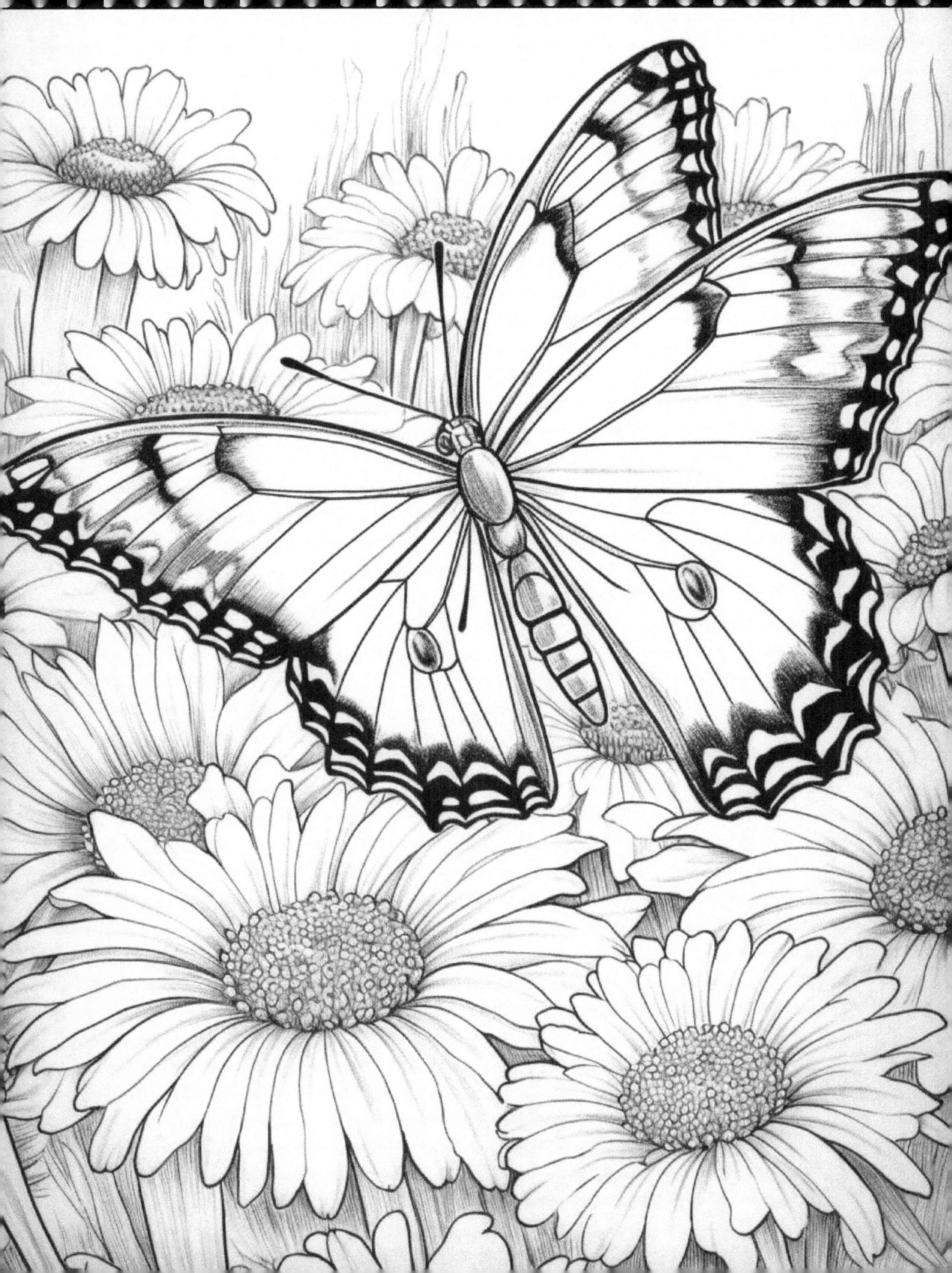

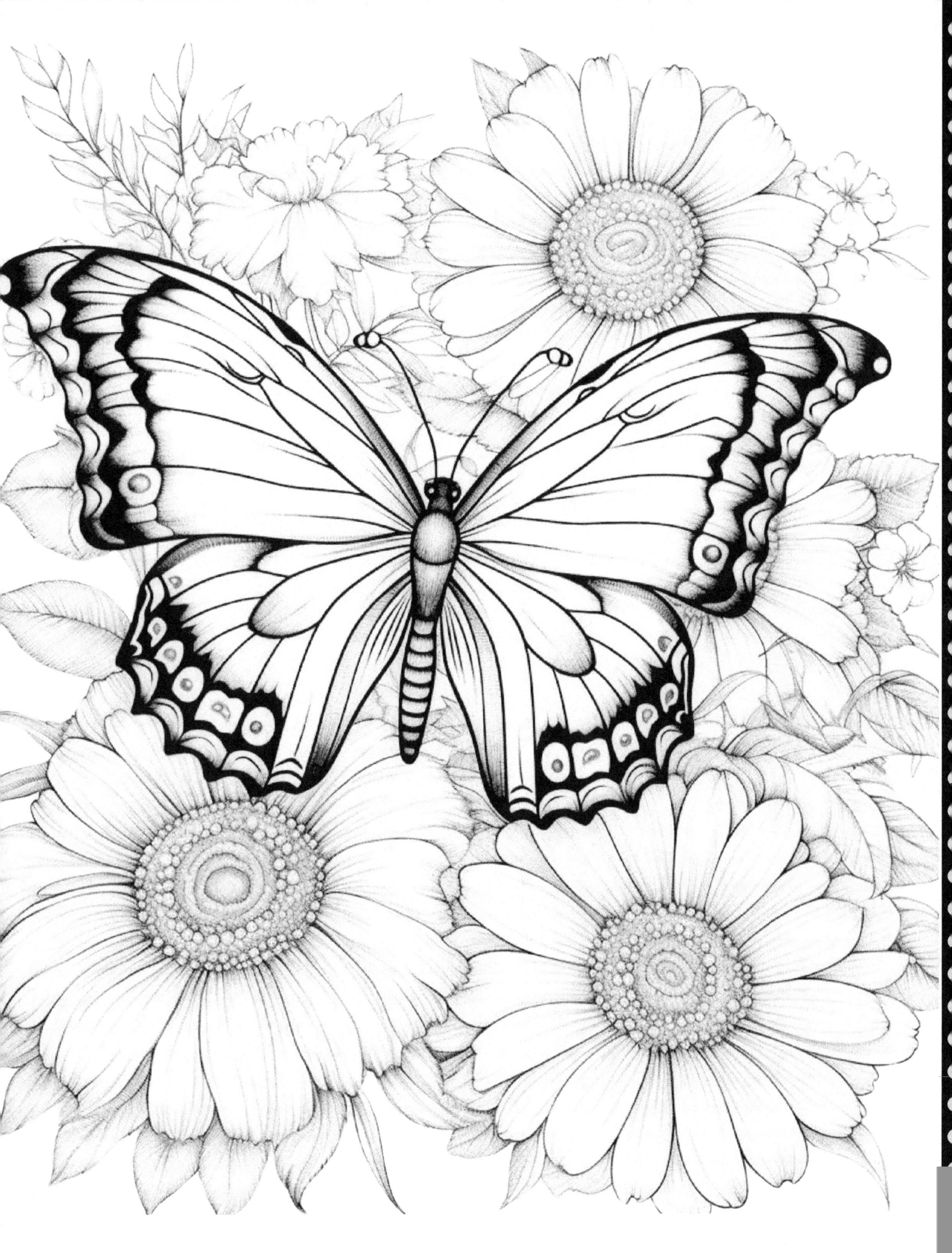

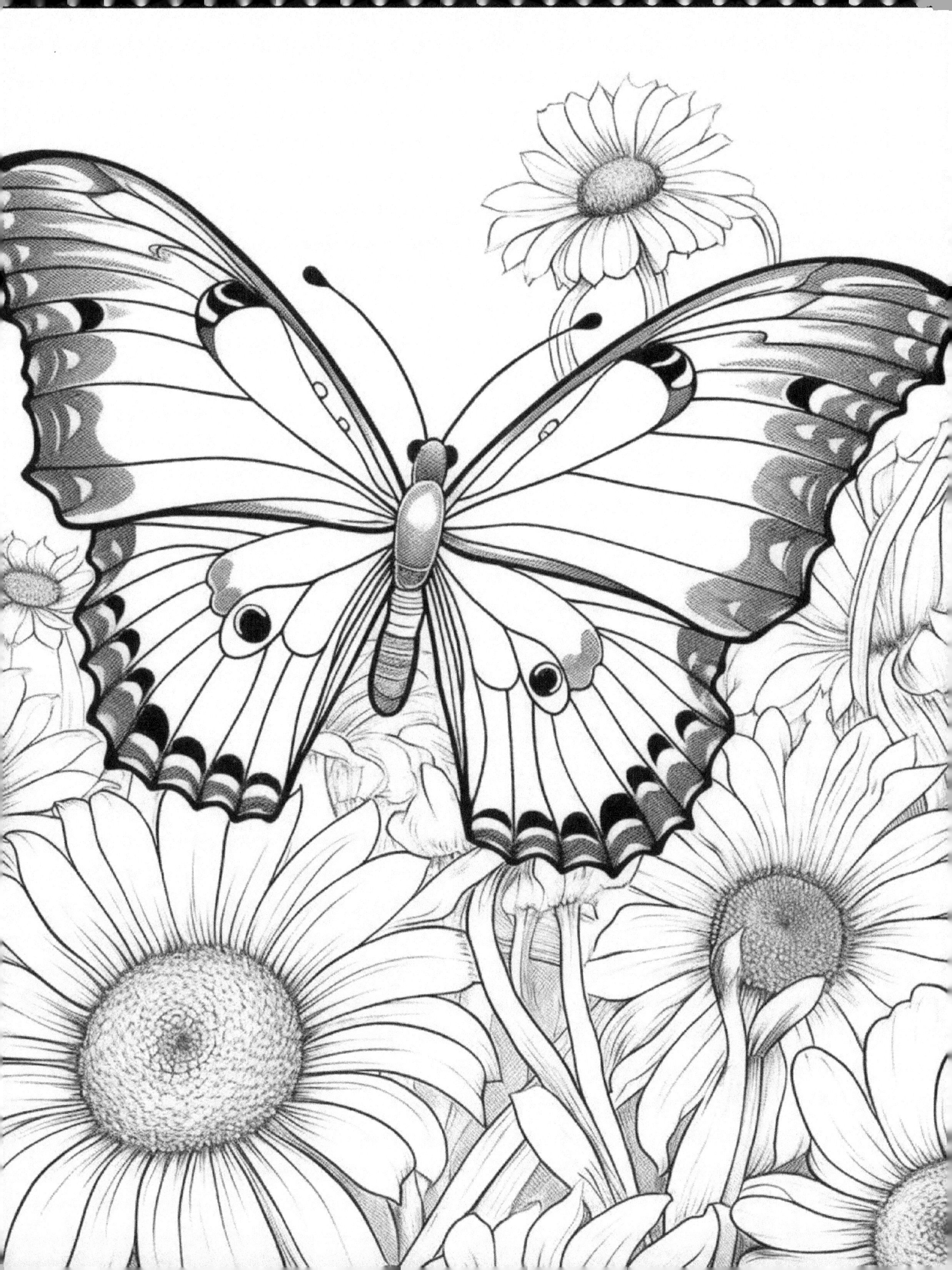

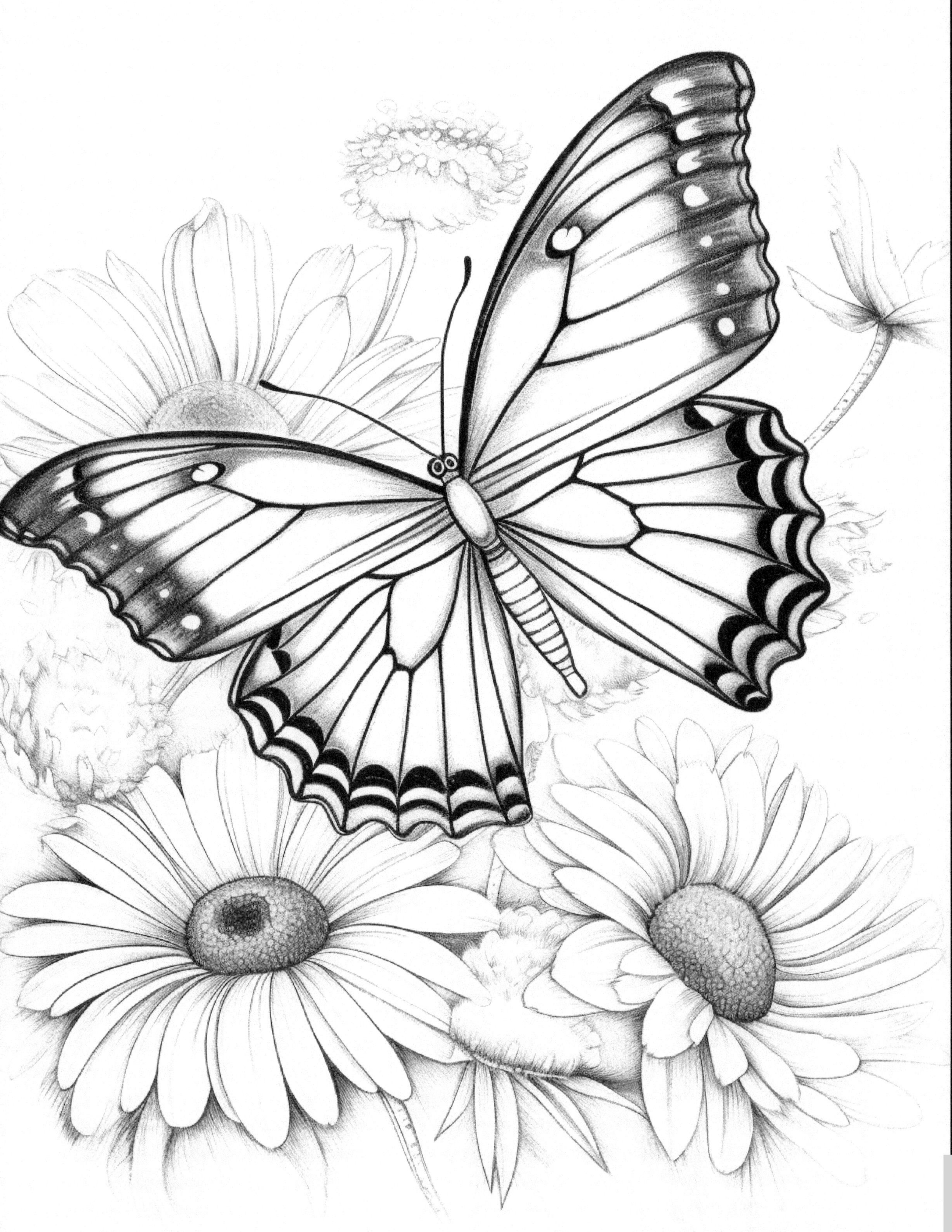

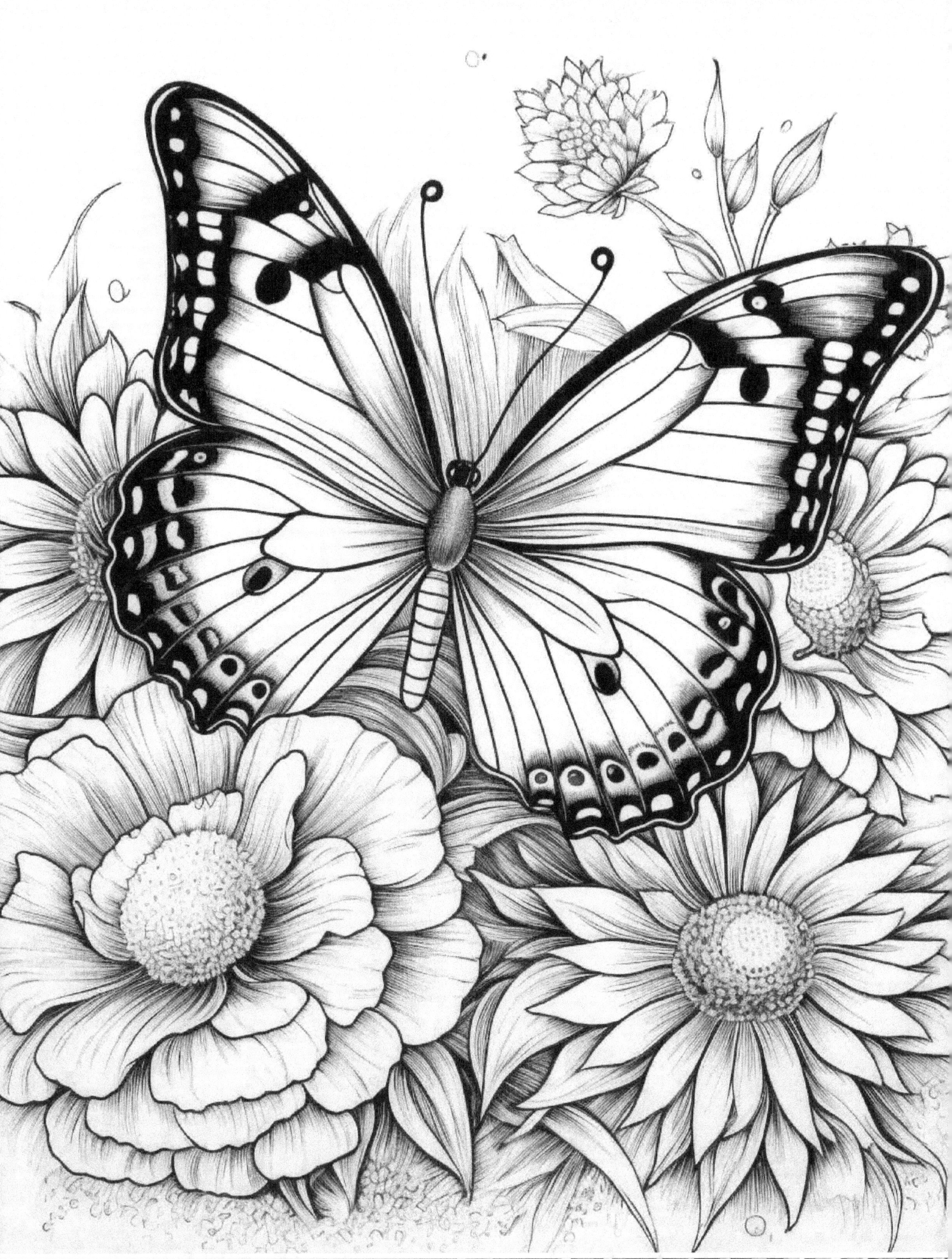

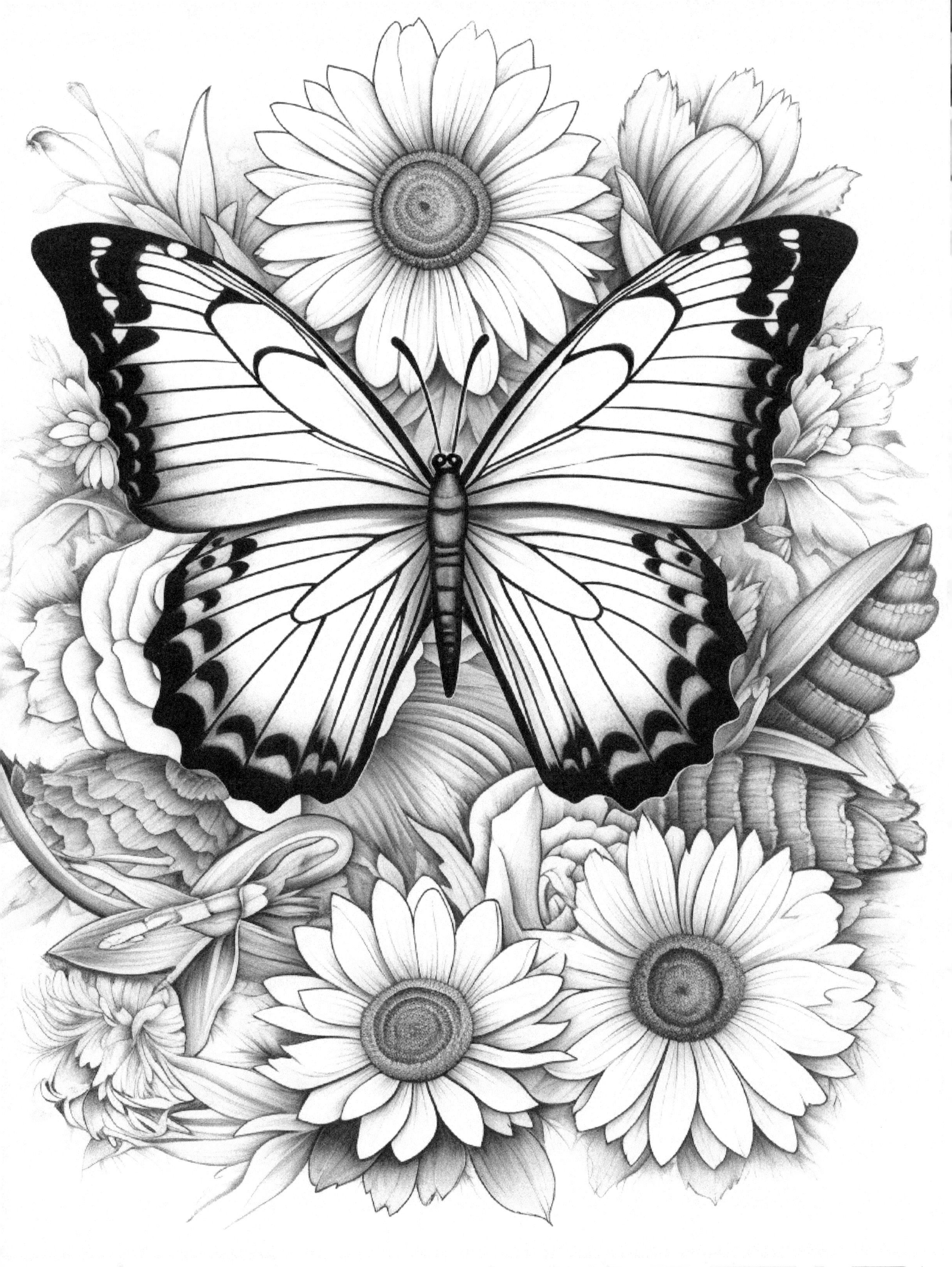

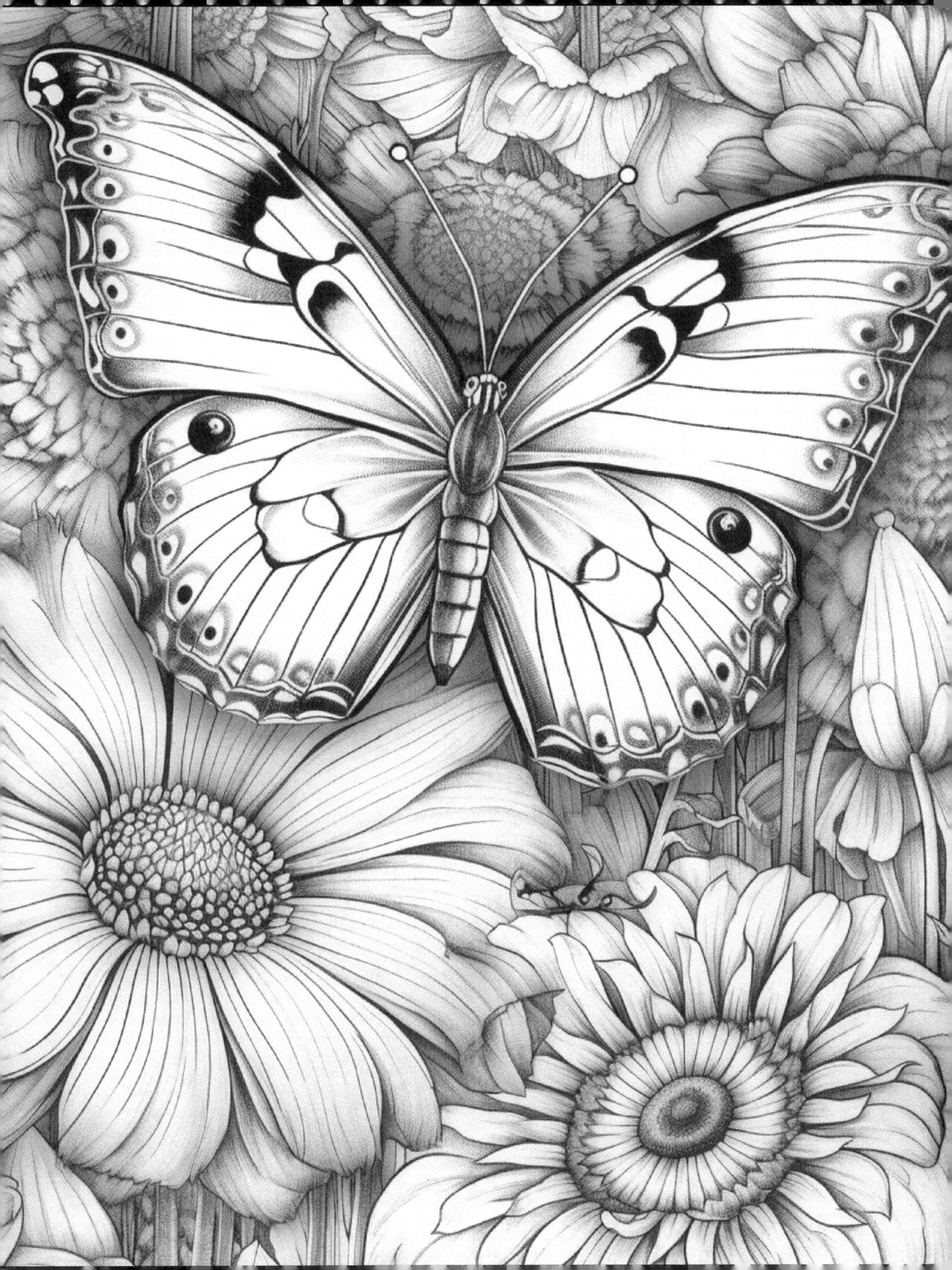

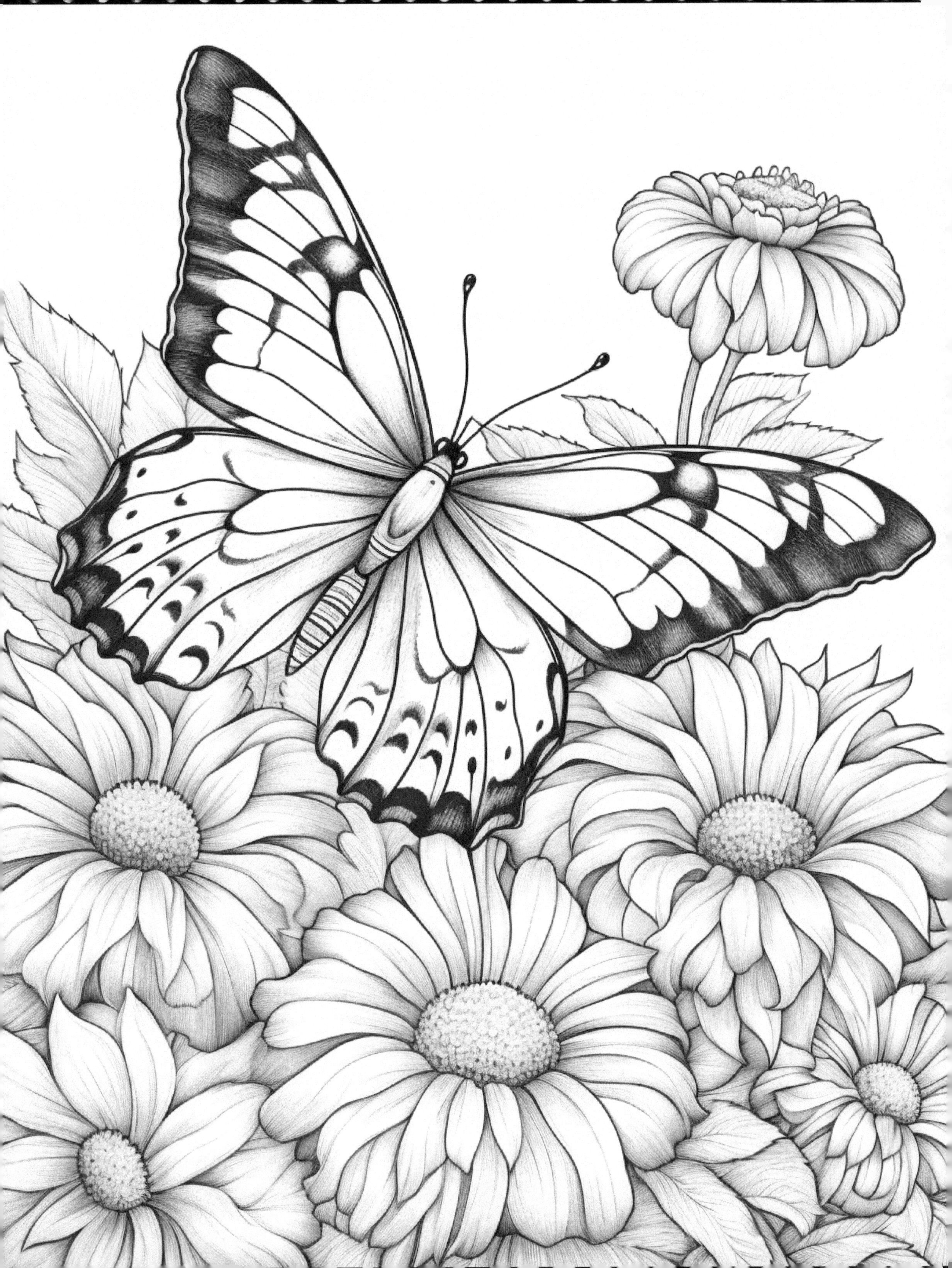

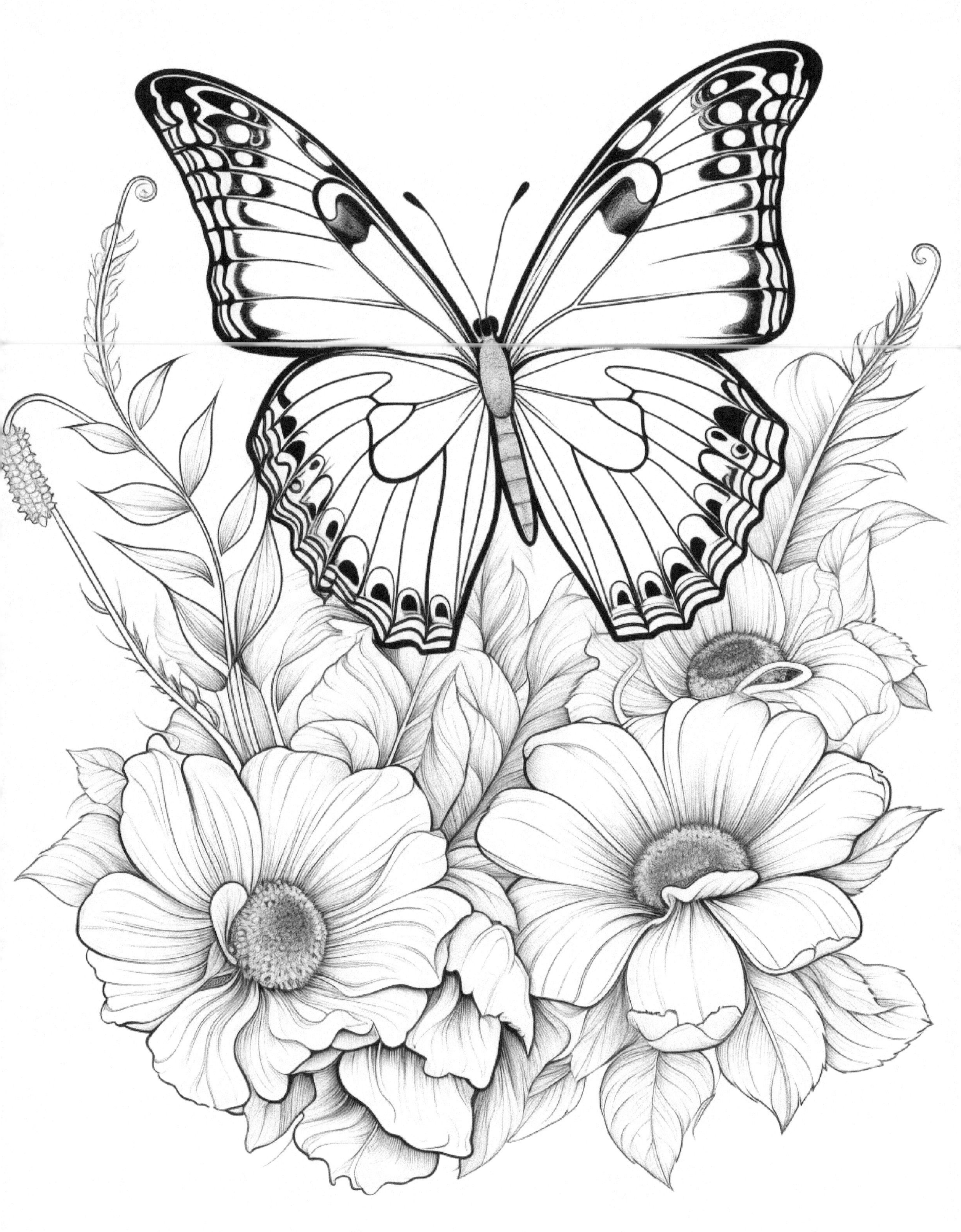

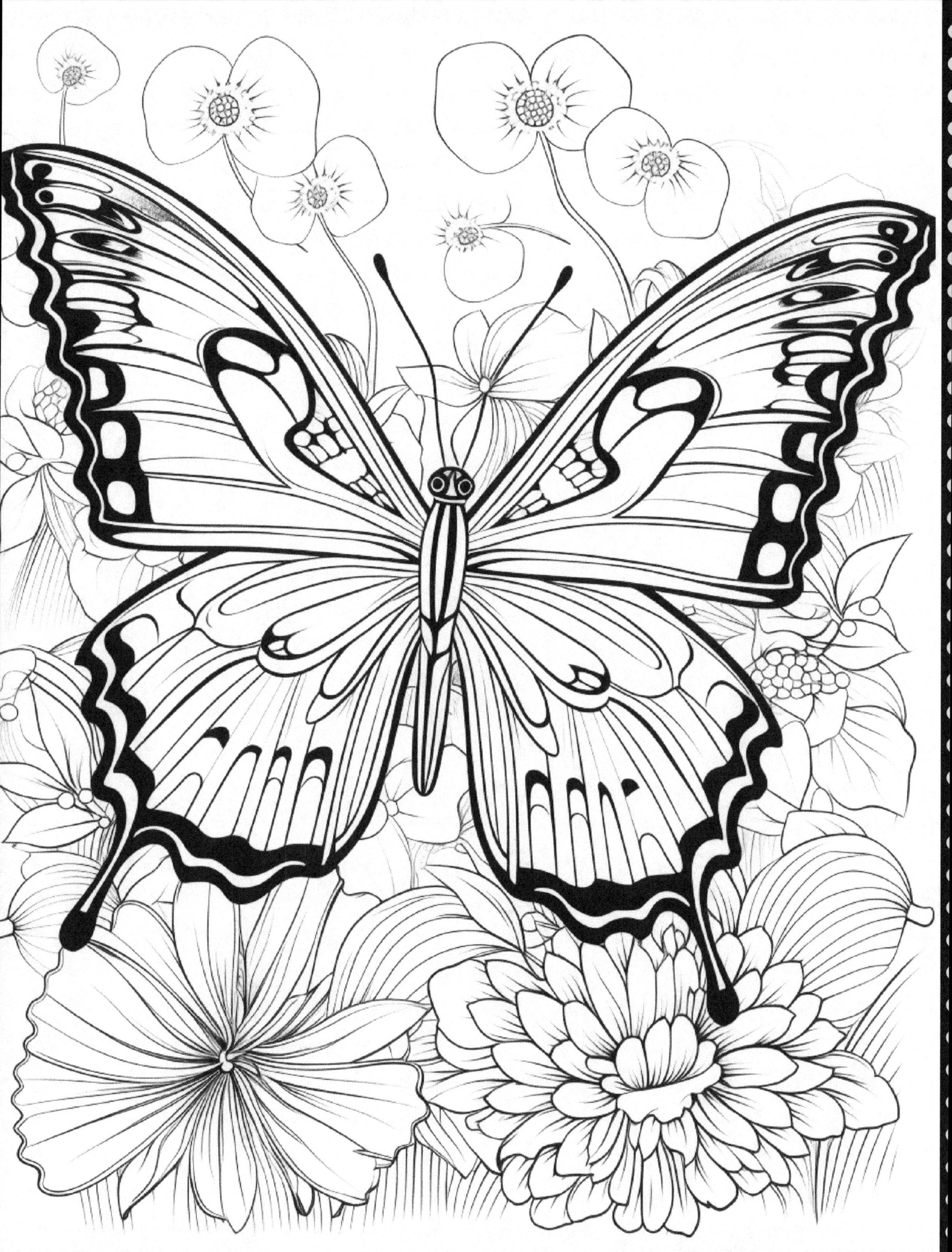

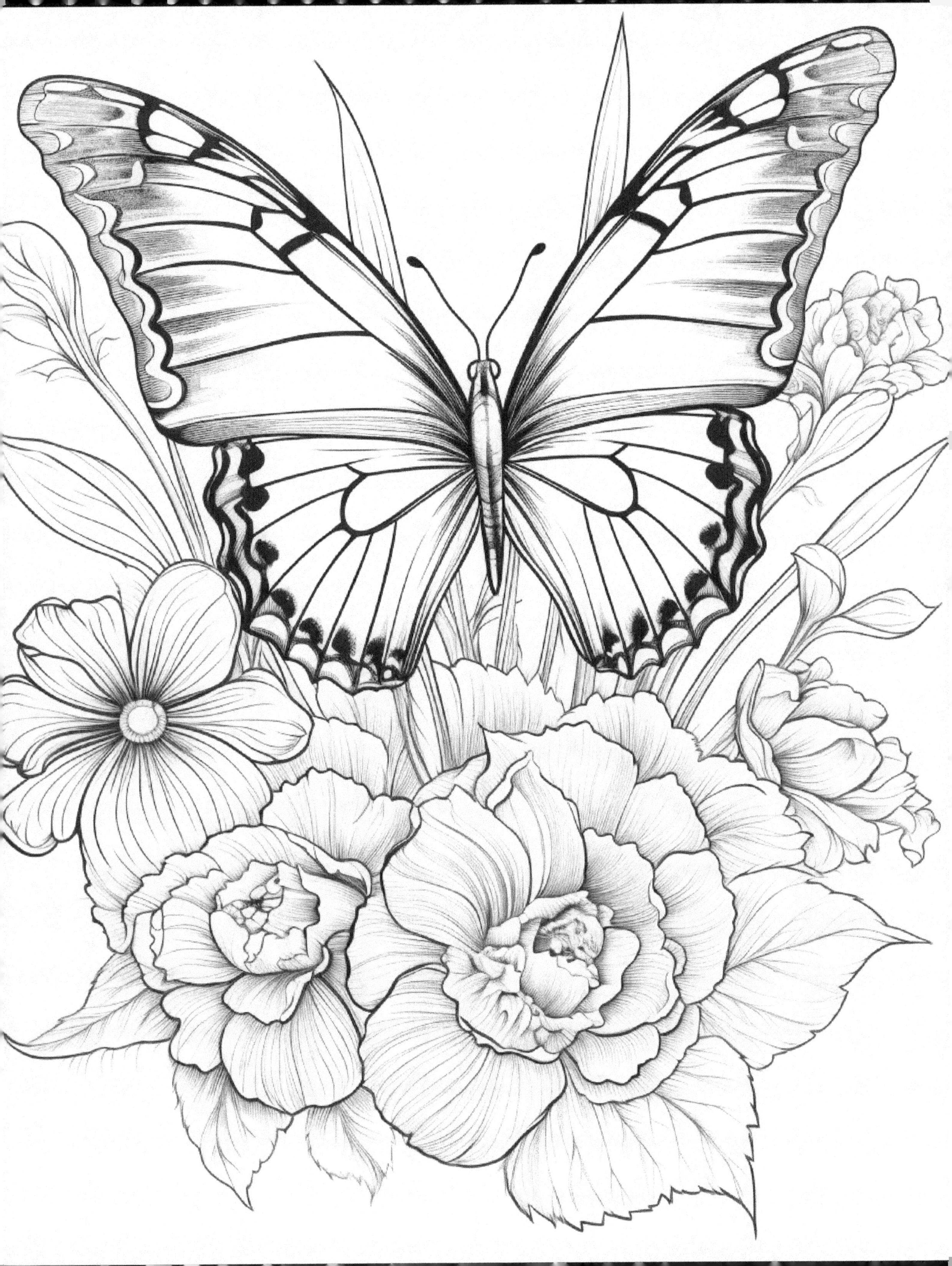

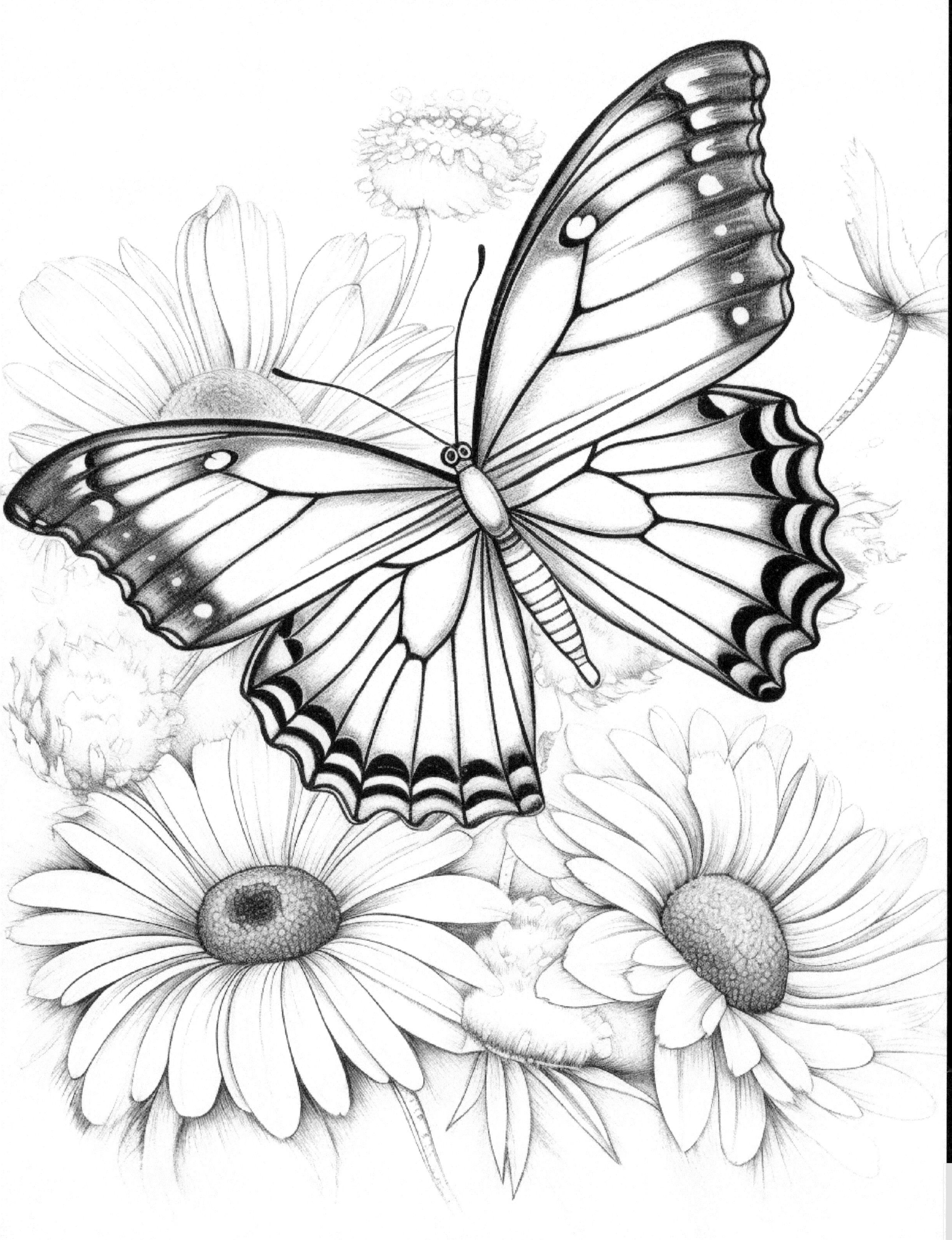

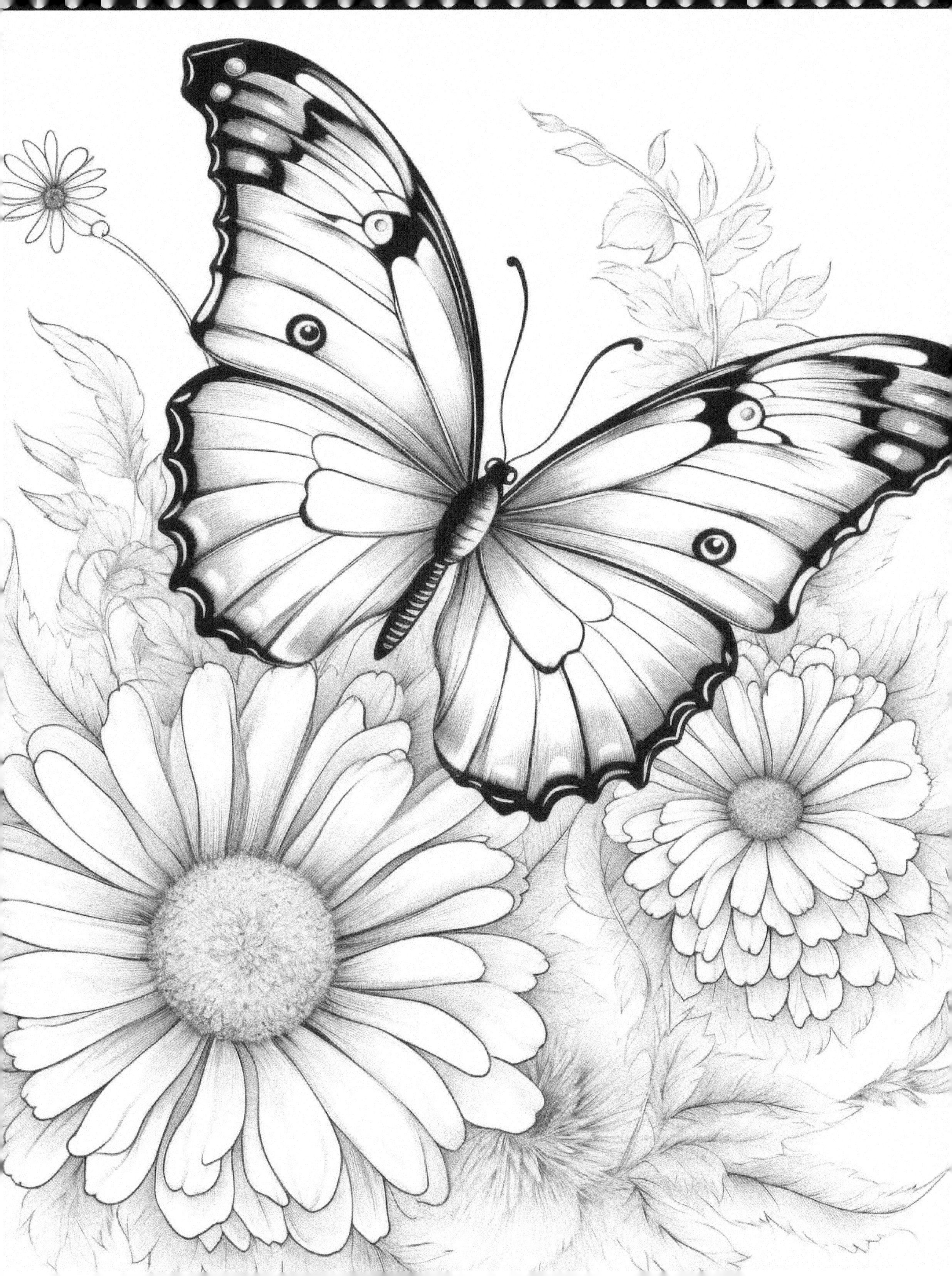

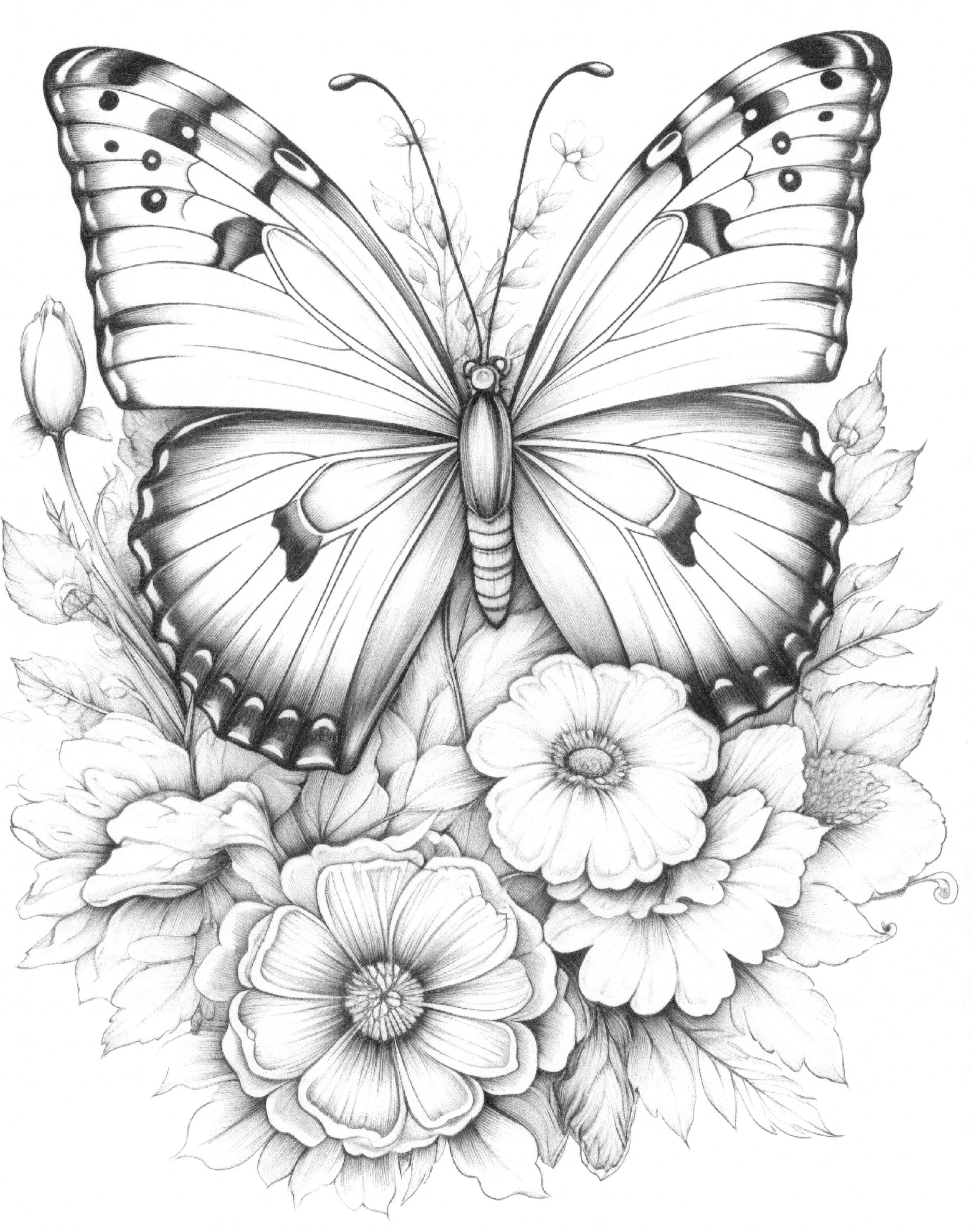

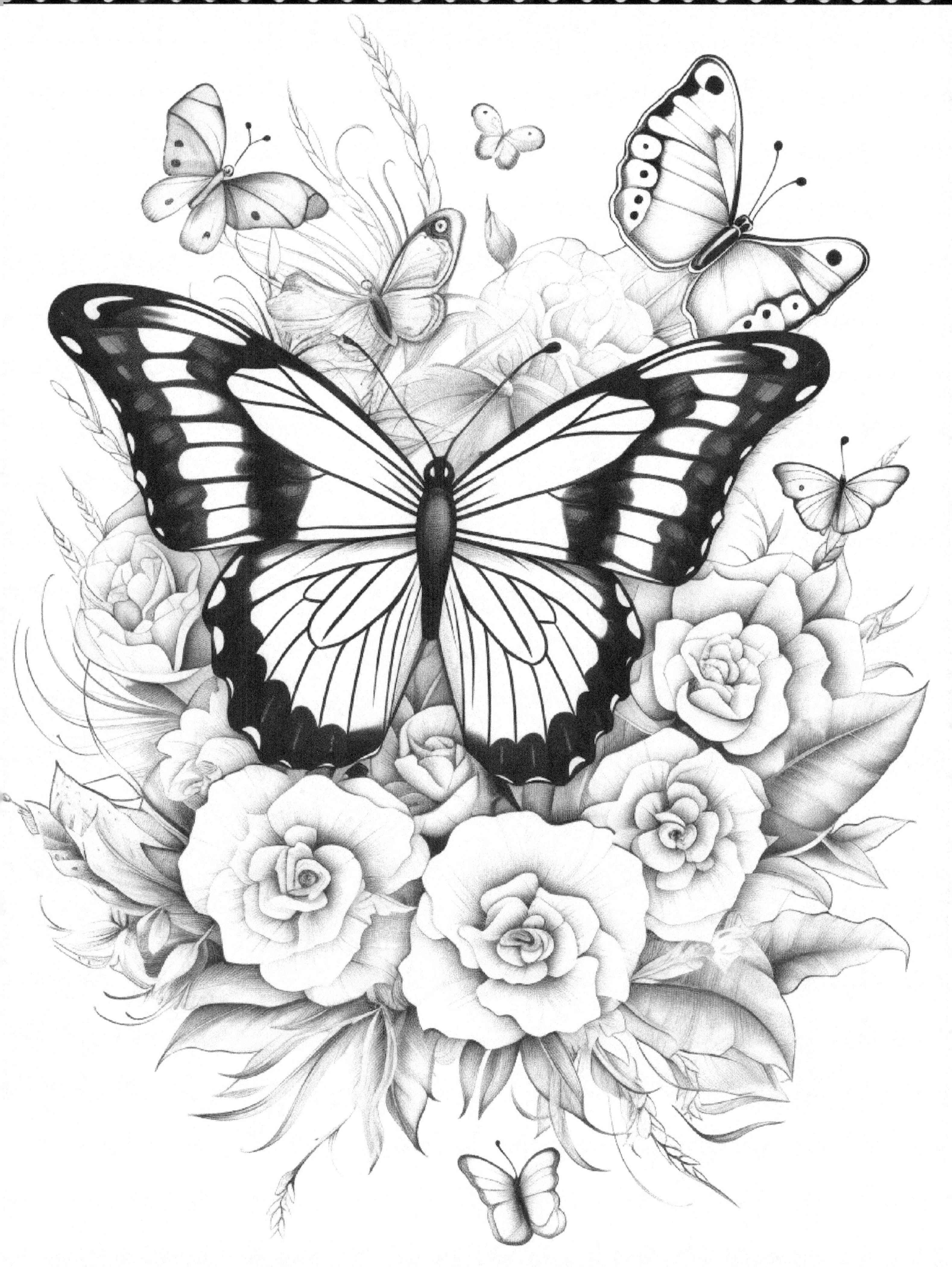

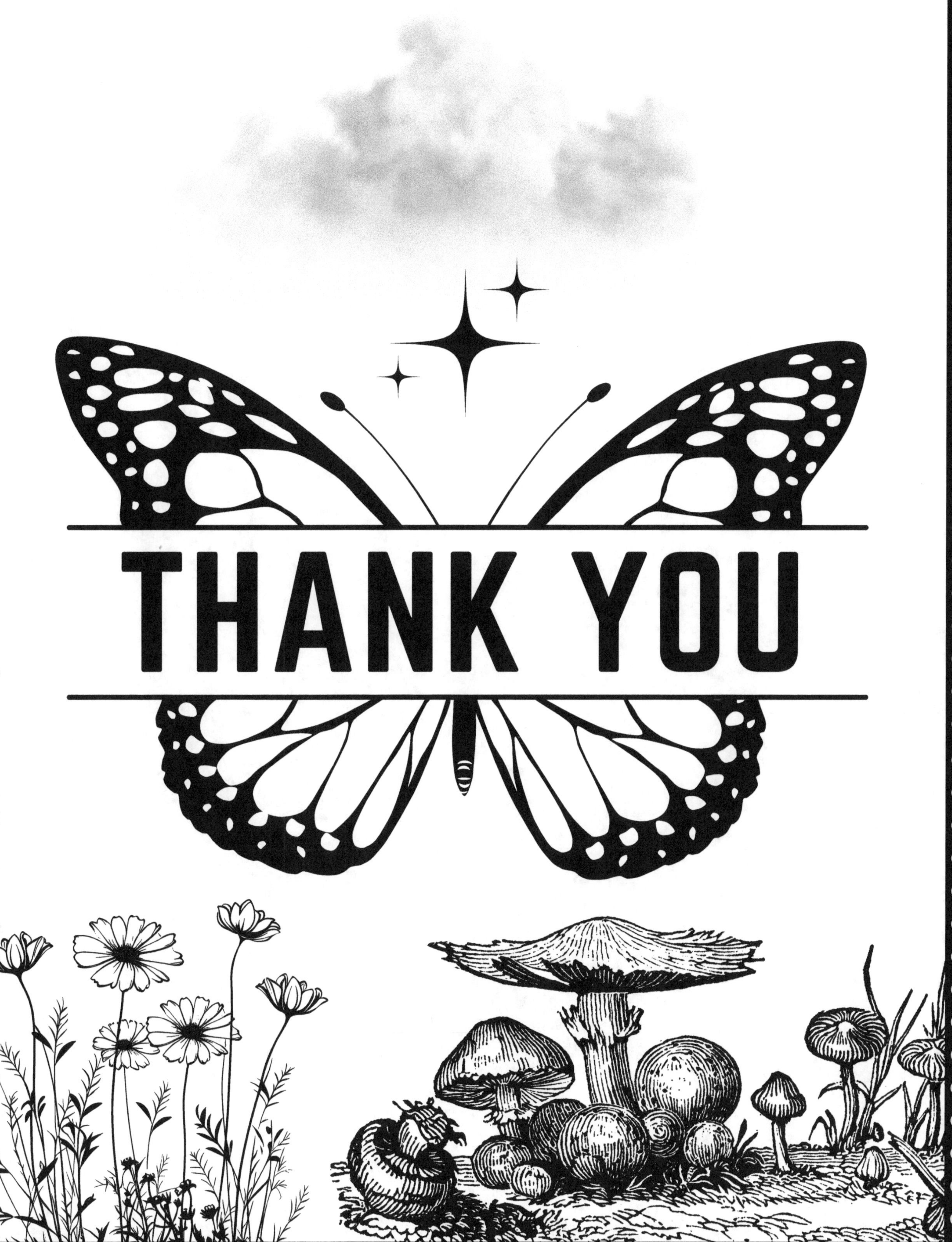
THANK YOU

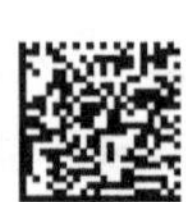